TWIN DAKOTAS

poetry and prose

Paul Beech

For Marie Lloyd,

Thank you for coming.

Hope you enjoy the book!

Very sincerely yours,

Cestrian Press

14/08/16

In memory of my wonderful parents,
Bert and Elsie Beech,
with love

First Published in 2016 by:
Cestrian Press
13, Stanton Road,
Bebington,
Wirral.
CH63 3HN

First Published 2016.

ISBN 978 0 904448 50 4

Printed and bound in Great Britain by:
Book Printing UK,
Remus House,
Coltsfoot drive,
Peterborough,
PE2 9JX

Contents

Acknowledgements   ix

Introduction   xi

Nature

Scallywags   17
Shag Tobacco   18
Haiku   19
Village After Rain   20
The Best Way   21
Haiku   22
Springtime   23
Upriver   24

Times Past

Twin Dakotas   27
Rituals   28
Mothballs   29
Pyjama Boys   30
The Dive   31
Robin   32
Could Have Been Us   33
Twilight   35
Nipper   36

Historical

The Wolf's Den 39

Stalemate 41

The Brave 44

Second Shadow 46

Displacement

Clandestines 51

The Old Majolica Bowl 54

That's All 56

Countdown 58

Too Much Blue 59

Sunday the Fiftieth of May 60

Later Life

Zafia 65

The Comet 68

Larkton Hill 69

Cappuccino 71

Talacre Beach 72

Contrasts

Poet Alone 77

Sputnik 78

City Siren 79

Royal Flush   80
Bandage   82
Cat Minding   84
Tanka   85
Bipolar   86
Haiku   88

Young Ones

Granny Red   91
Pollyanna-Dubček   93
The Pole   95
Aguila Gigante   96

Acknowledgements

I wish to thank the editors of the various publications in which some of these poems and prose pieces have previously appeared.

Scallywags – *Reflections, Issue 96*

Shag Tobacco – *Sons of Camus Writers' International Journal, Issue 12*

Haiku (black anvil cloud) – *50 Haikus, Issue 9*

Haiku (Ben Ledi), Tanka (Divine Radiance) – *Callander Haiku (Callander Press, 2016)*

Stalemate – *Lark Skies (Cestrian Press, 2015)*

Second Shadow, Could Have Been Us – *Sunlight Poems (Cestrian Press, 2016)*

Sunday the Fiftieth of May – *Rammenas, 2011*

Poet Alone – *Weekly World (Northwich, August 1980)*

City Siren – accepted for publication in *A Scream of Many Colours (Poetry Space, 2016)*.

Regarding the front and rear covers, thanks to Mike Penney for the photography and Kemal Houghton for the layout.

Thanks, Kemal, for all other assistance too, and to Caroline Wilson for proofreading.

Special thanks also to my partner Maureen Weldon for constant encouragement and bringing me out in the poetry world.

Introduction

As a lad I dreamt of becoming a writer like Conan Doyle or Ian Fleming, a poet like Dylan Thomas or Louis MacNeice. Well, so much for that! But I do have a book out now, this first collection of my poetry and prose, *Twin Dakotas*. And I'm very pleased. I've been writing seriously for 44 years, so it's been a long time coming.

My prose poem 'Twin Dakotas', after which this book is named, is about my wonderful late parents and was written whilst Dad was still alive. Bert and Elsie met at Powell's Milk Bar in Farnworth, Lancashire, during the Blitz year 1940, when he was 17 and she 15. The following year, upon turning 18, Bert enlisted with the RAF. They married following the war, in '46, and I was the first-born of their six children.

In 1972 I scored an early success with a children's story titled 'A Present for Pam', earning the princely sum of 75 pence from an animal welfare magazine – quite a surprise for Mum and Dad! Having no knowledge of the small presses where my work might have stood a chance, it was 1980/81 before I achieved publication again with four poems and an essay in a Northwich free newspaper of the day called *Weekly World*. And I shall never forget how delighted Mum and Dad were when I gave them copies. One of these poems was 'Poet Alone', which I've included here.

As a young dad in the latter '70s/early '80s, I entertained my children with tales made up in the telling and put a few of these down on paper when I got a chance between the increasing demands of my career in social housing. Following retirement, now a granddad, I revised or completely rewrote several – a sort of collaboration between my younger and older selves, quite fun! And I end this book with one of them, a quest story for older children, 'Aguila Gigante'.

The greatest compliment ever paid me was from Dad, when he told me I was very like Granddad Dawson. A Great War veteran decorated for bravery, Granddad Dawson became a policeman and rose to the rank of Chief Inspector. He was a talented self-taught violinist and during the Second World War, behind blackout curtains, would play accompanied by his two daughters, the younger, Elsie, my future mum. He was also a brilliant raconteur who in later life would draw on his experiences to hold us in thrall. Certainly any skill I possess for storytelling owes much to my granddad, and I've included two short poems about him here, 'Twilight' and 'Nipper'.

Several poems and stories stem from my career as a social housing manager. Working in a tough inner-city area: 'Sputnik' and 'City Siren'. Helping the homeless: 'That's All', 'Countdown', 'Too Much Blue' and 'Sunday the Fiftieth of May'. And three poems stem from my new life with Maureen: 'Larkton Hill', 'Cappuccino' and 'Talacre Beach'.

Mum and Dad's Twin Dakota clocks now hang on the wall above my computer, "just touching, kissing," as Dad would always say. What they'd have made of my book, I really don't know. But I've dedicated it to their memory with love.

Paul Beech,
May 2016

Nature

Scallywags

Nice morning, soft blue,
cheeky beaks at my window;
the sparrows are back.

Chirpy scallywags
gossiping in the laurel;
quick wings beat the air.

Nice morning, soft blue,
I feel like a boy again.
Aye, the sparrows are back.

Shag Tobacco

A wisp of shag tobacco, perhaps?
A balloon adrift in the valley,
self-esteem a snapped mooring.

So the willowed water's edge I wander,
sun glaring from plankton depths,
brain percolating,
florescent fungus twitching with broom.

Humble I connect.
Proud and the poetry eludes me.
A wisp of shag tobacco, perhaps?

Haiku

black anvil cloud
meteors spark
church bells ring

~~

sunrise
on rusty roof
I glide with gulls

~~

a lonely brook
leaves float by
first lanterns lit

Village After Rain

Cowering still from the downpour, the village holds its breath. Gullies gurgle full-bore. Friesians belch in the shippen. Otherwise all is silence. Pint-pots in hand, sawdust underfoot, the saloon-bar regulars make a sorry tableau...

Now comes a spider with bright legs to straddle the valley. Doors open and the village breathes again. Friesian methane mingles with the tang of the earth...

Don't anyone strike a match!

The Best Way

Why that way, towards the hills,
towards that blinding line as the sun sets,
skein after skein, honking?
Why not out across the sea?
I walk the Old Quay, wondering.

Waders cry in the flashing fire of the saltmarsh.
The glowing sandstone of the low wall
thrums with ancient knowledge.
Yet it is in your high-altitude honking
I find an answer:

Instinct, trust in instinct, it's the best way…

I take her hand in mine
and we sing.

Haiku

Ben Ledi dwarfs the town
stone brow riven with wisdom –
a cloud-shadow kiss

~~

sea-mist through tall trees
logs against tumbledown shed –
we sip red wine

~~

special still this place
rainbow in waterfall spray –
we climb to glory

Springtime

Tangled toads at water's edge,
male mallards vie for a female –
a girl and her granny laugh.

Upriver

A huge dog of Arctic origin bounds through the tussocks. His master squats on a stone. Across the river a conveyer clanks through an elevated tunnel connecting the old salt mine to its storage dome. An orange windsock dances in the stiff southwesterly and bedraggled flags flutter.

I'm watching a cormorant fly upstream when I feel the teeth. The huge dog has taken my right wrist between its jaws. His master is oblivious. The cormorant's wingtips clip the current as the teeth graze my skin.

The dog might have found my wrist in the field and now be offering it back.

"There's a good lad," I say, and he drops it.

a kindness
in the wolf's eyes
charms me

Times Past

Twin Dakotas

He bought them when she went into the nursing home with Alzheimer's, twin clocks in oak surrounds, Daniel Dakotas. Perfectly synchronised, the clocks would tick away their hours of slumber – his, greeting the eye when he awoke in the bed they'd shared nigh on sixty years; hers, reflecting that golden smile from the security of her cot sides. There'd be moments, bound to be, when the identical clocks would hold their simultaneous attention, like a lovers' moon.

Her clock was returned to him following the funeral, and with great care and a ball-peen hammer he hung it next to his own, just touching: "kissing", as he'd always say.

Frail and bent, trousers hitched around his ribcage on braces, he's in a home himself now, the twin Dakotas gone from his mind. He's seventeen years old, she fifteen, as they dance the blacked out streets of their small northern town, a raid in progress. The rattle and bounce of falling shrapnel becomes the mid-morning tea trolley. Old ladies dunk biscuits as he gathers her into the shelter of a milliner's doorway. Her golden smile is a promise that will never be broken.

Rituals

"My word,
you've got big feet!"
So you'd greet me grinning;
grip and kiss my hand on parting.
Cheers, Dad.

Mothballs

Buried with mothballs at the bottom of the chest,
an old blue uniform from the war,
an RAF uniform with two stripes,
my dad's.

Taller than my dad but still a boy,
I'd put it on and dream
of faraway battles and bravery.

In one pocket a packet of letters
from his sweetheart my mum
and his own tiny mother,
words I was never meant to read,
secrets I was never meant to know.

I'd replace the uniform carefully,
mothballs and all.

No one was ever the wiser.

Pyjama Boys

A black iron range, coals glimmer and glow;
three boys in pyjamas, they watch TV,
cosy with westerns, war, crumpets, cocoa…

A black iron range, coals glimmer and glow;
two brothers, their friend, sixty years ago,
now Christmas card names, across the country…

A black iron range, coals glimmer and glow;
three boys in pyjamas, they watch TV…

The Dive

Down "The Dive"
we felt alive,
back in '59.

Satchels dumped, ties askew,
we were grammar school boys
from up the cobbled hill,
fresh-faced still
but keen.

Nettle beer, cold and sweet,
jukebox belting out the beat,
we'd pose with fags unlit
and try our luck
with the girls.

Caught, we'd be for it next day,
teeth gritted against "The Whack",
determined not to crack,
shed a tear
or scream.

Down "The Dive"
we felt alive,
back in '59.

Robin

We were never best mates,
you made that very plain,
how well I remember your disdain.

You were a wild lad, Robin.
wild on your motorbike
in those distant days of The Cavern.

Leather-clad and devil-may-care,
you laughed at our warnings,
our promise of flowers for your funeral;
two fingers to Fate as you roared away,
Bader after Messerschmitts.

It was unbelievable when you died, Robin,
died the front-seat passenger in your best mate's car.
But we kept our promise.

Could Have Been Us

Two Boys in a Boat,
they could have been us, Bro,
the boys we were so long ago,
they could have been us.

In their boat ELIZA,
they gaze out to sea,
the standing boy in white shirt,
trousers rolled, me;
the seated boy in floppy hat,
oar hung over stern, you.
Aye, they could have been us, Bro,
could have been us.

I'd have been looking out
for gannets and skuas,
you for passing ships,
but the far horizon
would have drawn our joint attention
as we pondered the unknowable future,
brothers true,
best friends too.
Never would we have dreamt
of anything coming between us:
never, no, would we have dreamt it, Bro,
never back then.

So close all our lives
until now,
I'd bring you here if I could
to view this oil on canvas
by George Percy Jacomb-Hood,
Two Boys in a Boat.

Aye, they could have been us, Bro,
the boys we were so long ago,
they could have been us,
could have been us.

*AUTHOR'S NOTE: Painted by Jacomb-Hood in 1887, 'Two
Boys in a Boat' hangs in the Lady Lever Art Gallery, Port
Sunlight, Wirral.*

Twilight

Proud and true,
a church spire rises
against the churning, charging legions
of storm cloud.
In twilight glory,
nacreous clouds of rainbow hue
float in the higher regions beyond.

Snowdrops prick the earthly shadows,
his favourite spring flower always.
Proud and true,
with ginger tache and blue eyes,
decorated for bravery in the trenches,
he was my granddad.

Nipper

A nipper held high,
I told my granddad:
"The wind took my kiss away."

Historical

The Wolf's Den, Erddig

Lupus, nine centuries on I come for you. And what better place to start my search than here, two wolves carved from sweet chestnut, one howling, the other on its belly, brooding over crossed paws.

The Wolf's Den, this natural play area beneath tall trees, was named after you, Hugh d'Avranches, Norman overlord, scourge of the Welsh: 'Hugh the Wolf' (Hugh Lupus) so called for your savagery in the King's cause, 'Hugh the Fat' for your gluttonous bulk…

kiddies swing and climb
wild garlic the tang
of ancient bloodshed

The cry of a buzzard, the song of Black Brook. I feel the cool breath of Big Wood and go in search of your motte-and-bailey fortress with its scarps and ditches: Wristleham Castle, as probably known in your dark days of old. Only the earthworks remain, your timber towers long since perished and gone.

Deep in the woods I find you, glowering down from the gnarled bole of a medieval oak. And I steel myself before your true visage.

Lupus, in the name of God, *be gone!*

Author's Note: Erddig is an historic country home near Wrexham, North Wales, now in the ownership of the National Trust. Hugh d'Avranches (Lupus) was born c1047, became the First Earl of Chester 1071 and died 27 July 1101, four days after becoming a monk.

Stalemate

Introduction

Charles Hamilton Sorley was born in Aberdeen on 19 May 1895, son of William Ritchie Sorley, a professor at Aberdeen University, and his wife Janetta. Charles had a twin brother, Kenneth, whom he would always be close to. The family moved to Cambridge when he was five.

Charles attended King's College Choir School, then Marlborough College, where he won prizes for English and Public Reading. In 1913, he gained a scholarship to University College, Oxford, but prior to taking this up went to Germany to study the language and culture. Upon the outbreak of World War I, he was interned in Trier but released after one night and told to leave the country.

Despite his affection and admiration for the German people, he enlisted with the Seventh Battalion of the Suffolk Regiment. He arrived in France as a Lieutenant in May 1915 and was quickly promoted to Captain. He fell whilst leading his men at the Battle of Loos on 13 October 1915, shot in the head by a sniper. He was just 20 years old.

Thirty-seven complete poems were found in his kit following his death, and in 1916 a posthumous collection, Marlborough and Other Poems, was published to great acclaim.

On 11 November 1985, Charles Hamilton Sorley was one of sixteen First World War poets commemorated on a slate stone unveiled in Poets' Corner, Westminster Abbey.

***

Prose Poem

Gas, smoke, the thunder-rush of shells.

The eagle-eyes of the sniper miss nothing. A brave son of the Fatherland, we'll call him Fritz.

Mid-afternoon, the British are through the wire and at the trench now, bayonets flashing. And leading with his pistol is an officer…

Captain Charles Sorley of the Suffolks is another brave man, a man with Germany in his heart yet ready to die for England.

Camouflaged, concealed, Fritz levels his rifle. Will he be haunted by that face, by a momentary impression of dutiful youth and kinship?

Here is the cheerful chatterbox kid who loved beachcombing with his twin-brother. Here, the Marlborough College student who loved running in the rain and excelled in debate; the young man of social conscience who worried about the poor, who travelled Germany, even felt himself German, and was entertained in his lodgings by a half-tame squirrel. Here is Sorley the unsentimental, truthful poet of the war.

Not that Fritz knows any of this as gently he squeezes the trigger and adds another to his tally. Tomorrow the battle will end in stalemate.

***

Charles Hamilton Sorley,
dead at twenty,
body never recovered,
poetry never forgotten.

The Brave

Extracts from the diary of an Old Soldier, long since deceased:

Tuesday 16.vii.18, Netley Hospital

So many times have I followed the bayonet, Gerry bullets singing in my ears, the thunder-rush of shells bursting orange in mud & guts, yet nary a scratch sustained. Oh, the irony of it, that a micro-organism should have caused my languishing here, in the company of one whose injury – as confided to me, & contrary to the official findings – was not so much accidental as self-inflicted, a contemptible "Blighty Wound."

Aye, but I am guilty too, despite my citation and Military Medal: guilty of surviving good pals on the line. So when, this morning, with a broken piece of cup, the wretch did hack at his wrists, it was with some rage I stopped him. "Nay, laddie, that is not the way," I bellowed. "Give o' ye best & be a man, damn you!"

The nurse came bustling at my summons, so pure of countenance and gentle her brogue that I thrilled as my pals in Picardy will no more. Her name is Bridget & between us, surely, we have an understanding of sorts...

Tuesday 30.v.44, Larkin Lodge

So long has it been, I am almost beyond hope. Oh Rosslyn, dearest daughter, with your lovely face pure as your late Irish mother's, your gentle voice musical too. Seven weeks – aye: seven weeks, three days, six hours, thirty-two minutes. The rain came pelting earlier; now each passing second is marked by the slow drip of the gutter.

I press your knitting to my face, your every loving stitch a wonder. They wanted you away, didn't they? France again, of course, to work with the Marquis by moonlight, with stealth & purpose, a fortune in francs on your head no doubt, that volume of poetry your constant companion & talisman.

It is time – time to summon my courage & open the package that arrived this morning by some mysterious means. I fumble, the brown paper rips...& nay, I am not mistaken: it's the Rimbaud.

"Elle a été trahie en Picardie," runs the anonymous note enclosed. She was betrayed in Picardy.

Mrs B brings watercress sandwiches on a tray & tucks a napkin under my chin.

Oh Rosslyn...

***

The Old Soldier received official word exactly one week later, on Tuesday 6th June 1944 – D-Day.

Second Shadow

Born of a swamp it was,
a swamp and the vision to reclaim it,
the grand vision of a businessman.

A Bolton businessman of the Victorian Age,
William Hesketh Lever
dreamt of retiring to a Scottish isle
but chose a new venture instead:
the manufacture of soap.

Born of a swamp it was,
this place of architectural wonder
and philanthropic zeal,
     a factory for honest toil,
     a garden village for the workers,
this place of blackboards and belfry
and artworks aplenty,
of birdsong, squirrel and bloom:
Port Sunlight on the Mersey.

Extinguished twice would the sunshine be,
by the drear shadow of the First World War,
then again by the shadow of the Second.
Mercifully gone was he,
long before that moonlit night in '41
when, with a single bomb,

the Luftwaffe flattened shops and homes
in this village of peaceful green.

Born of a swamp it was,
this place of vision and virtue.
Now Hitler sought to destroy it.

Pray God there is no Third Shadow.

Displacement

Clandestines

We came ashore stinking of fish from our nightmare crossing in the traffickers' trawler, those of us who survived, that is. A woman drowned and a small boy died in the bows.

How the others fared, those poor souls from the ruins of our war-torn land, God knows. I made it to the forest and slept two nights in a rockwall crevice, frozen and starved, before they came for me with chopper and dogs.

Miraculously, a learned man no more but a hunted animal with primitive instincts, I gave them the slip, blatting rotor-blades and canine yelps fading as I waded through mud, scrambled through thickets of thorn, vaulted fences and walls, then jumped a train. Now here I am in the town where my sister, a "clandestine" too, lives with seedy friends who demand favours to keep her safe.

They live in an upstairs flat near the estuary, that's all I know. But find her I must. I'm all she's got. And in her last call before we lost contact she sounded afraid, terribly afraid.

***

A week later, rotor-blades again. Choppers, two of them, like giant dragonflies over the moonlit estuary and town, one with a peevish whine, the other a thudding drone, as they hover, move on, hover, move on, around and around, searching with thermal imaging cameras, searching for me…

With a half-eaten burger from a bin, I'm back in my hiding place above a ventilation duct in an underground car park, empty at this hour except for an old jalopy with flat tyres. Night after night I've lain here, in this pre-cast concrete tomb, shuddering in my stolen coat, munching bin-pickings, worrying about my little sister.

Not one glimpse of her in all my riverside wanderings, her phone dead, maybe smashed by the thugs she's living with. Her sweet face haunts me. Her poor, stricken, dust-covered face when I saw her last, months ago, following the missile strike that destroyed her home. I'm all she's got, her only hope. But they're closing in on me now. Sirens, flashing blue lights. The police, Immigration Enforcement, they're closing in.

***

They charge up the ramp as I exit near the Market Hall and plunge into the maze of alleyways leading down to the quay. A swarthy, brutish, leering face at an upstairs window as I round a corner. A woman lies battered, bloodied and broken on the cobbles. She is conscious, but only just. I have found my sister.

Kneeling at her side, I'm cocooned in a beam of intensely bright light from a hovering chopper, the peevish one.

"Stand back from that woman," commands an amplified voice from above.

I kiss her brow. She is trying to say something.

"Stand back from that woman – *now!*"

A hoarse whisper: "You came…"

"I'm here," I say. "Right here, Little Sis, right here…"

Rough hands seize me from behind. But there is a moment's worth of mercy at least. Her eyes glaze and Little Sis departs this sorry world for a higher realm where all are welcome, a realm without clandestines.

Unresisting, I am pulled to my feet and marched to a waiting van.

The Old Majolica Bowl

She's just a little girl, my love.
She cannot speak nor even cry,
so terrible have been
the things she's seen
in her faraway ravaged land,
the land she has fled in fear.
But she's just a little girl like you.

No mummy, daddy or granny anymore
because of the war,
she lives in a muddy camp across the Channel.

All she has left is an old Italian bowl,
the gloriously coloured majolica bowl
that always stood in a shaft of light,
lemons, limes and apples piled bright.
It's a miracle it wasn't destroyed by the bomb.
Pity anyone who'd steal it now
for this little girl can be fierce.

She paints like you, my love,
but uses more red than blue,
much more red than you.
She cannot speak but paints in red.

In her cold camp bed
she clutches her bowl,

the old majolica fruit bowl.
Miracles do happen,
and cross the Channel she will someday
to a happy life in our country.
Kind people to care for her
and a little girl who will be her friend,
a friend who'll help her find her voice again.
So she believes.

A little girl like you, my love.

That's All

(a true story)

Midnight, silence, frost glistening under the moon. He slows for the junction at the top of the hill.

As if from nowhere, a woman lurches into the road. There is something very wrong with her. She is barefoot, wearing only a thin pink dress, near collapse. Her face is contorted in a way he has never seen before, eyes desperate in his headlights.

He gets out. She is shaking and wailing in extreme distress, pleading for help.

Somehow he gets her into the car. "Have you done something?" he asks, meaning to herself.

"Done something? Done something? I've been beaten, that's all."

Upon arrival at the infirmary, porters help her into a wheelchair. And for the first time he notices the hideous black bruising to her legs.

"What will people think?" she says. "I've been beaten, that's all...that's all..."

***

Many years on, retired now, he is haunted still by the look in her eyes, and her words...those words. He became a social housing manager and the work he always loved best was helping the homeless, especially victims of domestic violence. That young man was me.

Countdown

Midnight in bed,
and a whirling, rustling spiral of dreams,
fragments of the day gone by,
dead leaves in a storm.

2 a.m.,
and a lingering whiff of witchcraft,
the smell of an old tramp,
woodfire for warmth in the snow.

4 a.m.,
and a hazy moon replicated on my pane,
ghostly eyes, accusing still:
"S'alright for you, Guv, you've gorra big 'ouse."

6 a.m.,
and downriver a cock crows,
time to do it all again, almost:
another day with the homeless.

Too Much Blue

Her unborn kicks as weary she rests on a frozen bench in a bleak northern town.

Seven hours have passed since she fled his fists with naught but the babe in her womb, the clothes on her back and a small knotted bundle. Seven hours of bus after bus, caring not where she went, only to pile up the miles behind her. He mustn't find her. Must never find her.

The darkening clouds have a purple tinge, a sure sign of snow. Strangers hurry by; crows croak in a foreign tongue. Across the road, outside the Town Hall, garishly lit with coloured lights, stands a Christmas tree.

A headscarf bobs before her. A withered hand points to a door. Her unborn kicks. Then stiffly she rises, bundle in hand.

Too much blue, she thinks, crossing. Too much blue.

O for a splash of gold.

Sunday the Fiftieth of May

She wakes to the buzz of a wasp behind the curtains, haggard, stale, mildly overhung. Pigeons call over the river. Something scratches her brain. It's Crystalmas Day, Sunday the fiftieth of May.

Muriel is the Warden at Watson's High Security Refuge, a big woman with a big heart.

Crystal is four years dead today. She was the only one of the Watson's women ever to have thrown her rug out. She'd loved the stone-slab solidity of the former farmhouse floor. She'd grind her feet into the grain of the stone until they bled; until, with blood, came belief.

"Ah, no boards," she'd cry, ecstatic. "No boards with cracks between. No cracks for an evil eye."

***

After three weeks at a guesthouse in the Highlands, Crystal had begun to hope. Safe at last – oh, if only...The rustling beneath the floor she'd put down to rats. Then she'd seen him peering up at her through a crack. Kevin...

He'd found her again.

In the protected environment at Watson's, two hundred miles south, in a remote rural location, the true Crystal gradually emerged. It did her good to tell the tale. She held the other women in thrall.

"I was right, there was a rat down there! A fixated, vicious rat. I loved to write poetry; Kevin destroyed my work. I loved to swim; he'd beat me for it. He couldn't swim himself, of course…"

Slightly built and quietly spoken, Crystal had a certain charisma. The women listened to her. They loved her. Muriel loved her too.

Bluebells her eyes and daffodils her hair,
Snowflakes clothed her soul.

So ran one of the poems in a little pamphlet Muriel printed for her.

Crystal's calendar was adopted by the women following her death. It worked on the countdown principle and gave hope in the long wait for a home.

When down The Hollow foxes play,
Rejoice, girls, for keys are on the way!

For Crystal, it had seemed the foxes would never play. Then one sweet Spring morning they did. She rejoiced with a dip in the river.

Muriel found her on the pontoon, dead, a young man weeping over her.

"Are you Kevin?"

Ten minutes later she rang the police on her mobile. She'd found two bodies, she said. Crystal, strangled. And a young man facedown in the water.

***

It's Sunday the fiftieth of May, Crystalmas Day. She sits in her garden at Watson's. Crystal is four years dead. The evening is fragrant with spring-flowers. She blows the open end of a half-drunk bottle of lager. The result is a passable pigeon call. A real pigeon calls back over the river.

The scratch in her brain has eased now.

Later Life

Zafia

She was sitting across the table, her back to the rain-spattered window, newspaper raised. Two or three unfortunates, who'd entered the reference library seeking shelter, sat either side of her but in a different world. It was a thin, Polish language newspaper, *Dziennik Polski*. I had no clear view of her face but her dimpled cheek and auburn hair brought a single name to mind – Zafia.

But how could this be?

***

Never have I known eyes so expressive, a smile so radiant, a voice so gently teasing. Zafia was our waitress at the Cornish hotel where my wife and I spent a week in the autumn.

One morning, the egg with my Traditional English Breakfast was over-done, bullet hard, just the way I like it. I'd beamed my preference to her telepathically, I said. Zafia's hand flew to her mouth, her look of astonishment so complete it was comic. Her colour rose as she failed to suppress a laugh. I laughed too and all at the table joined in. The dig in my ribs hurt. "Act your age," hissed Daphne, my wife. "You're old enough to be her dad!"

***

Cornwall, so rugged, colourful and poetic, was like nowhere we'd been before, and we loved it.

Zafia made our every meal special. Maybe we made her every service special too. We were amongst her last guests as she counted down the days to her own departure, her return to Kraków, her family, a new job in the media and her beloved myślinska sausages. She confided to me that she always ate these sliced on rye bread.

I felt bereft on the coach home. Still do really, though I try to hide it from Daphne. I picture Zafia in Kraków, wandering beside the Vistula River or through the Old Town. Does she ever think back to that dining room with green cloths on white covering the tables, a wall-length window presenting an often misty view of the bay below? Does she remember Table 22 and the way our eyes would sometimes meet?

***

Two of the beery-smelling men at her library table had fallen to telling lewd jokes, perhaps assuming she wouldn't understand. The third dozed over Debrett's *People of Today*. But the rain had ceased its drumming now and the mucky-minded ones hauled up their mate to drag him away.

"Zafia," I said at last, but there was no response.

I tried again: "Zafia." And this time the newspaper came down.

"My name is Wanda," she said.

Wanda? Her lipstick was startlingly red. Otherwise she was so like Zafia, she had to be a sister. Her eyes fizzed in amusement at my confusion.

"You are from Kraków?"

"Gdanśk," she said. Then, pointedly, with a little jerk towards the leaded pane behind her: "The sun, it shines…"

Her *Dziennik Polski* firmly back in place, I read the headline without comprehension before following the unfortunates out of the library and down the steaming street.

The Comet

Moonlight, daffodils, a weeping willow,
and in the northern sky a comet
with a ghostly tail. The letter
was my last hope, and time
was running out for a reply. Soon
the comet would be gone, my heart
with it.

Every night the mail tray,
checking and rechecking then stuffing
it all back, the comet a little lower,
a little brighter. Daffodils and dreams,
your voice and your tender smile.

Another full moon,
a spray of white blossom,
my footsteps hollow on the broken path.

Author's Note: My inspiration for this was the magnificent comet Hale-Bopp, which outshone all the stars in the sky except Sirius as it passed perihelion on 1st April 1997...

Larkton Hill

Steep is this track I climb
hand-in-hand with my love,
our friend leading the way
up this wooded shoulder of sandstone,
her jolly dog Spot racing by,
a skitter of paws in golden leaf.

Steep is this track of tangled briars,
mossy green boulders,
the flash of a jay,
milky mist threading through birch, holly, oak,
as far below lies the old life
where my ghost must reside in photographs hidden,
spoons in a drawer the wrong way round,
a certain chair claimed by others.

Steep was the climb to this high heath
of heather, scrub, adders,
buzzards aloft,
where we lunch on a log,
Spot, ears pricked, forepaw raised,
as the Iron Age ghosts of Maiden Castle
call me down.

Steep was the climb to this summons rejected,
sun breaking through over distant hills,
bright blood hot in my veins,
bubbling mirth,
an accidental selfie,
no ghost at all
as I claim this new life.

Cappuccino

Yesterday we sat outside a café.
Bunting danced behind our necks.
I drew closer,
made myself into a windbreak for her.
And chuckle she did, with her eyes.

My cappuccino was delicious
or maybe it wasn't:
I don't know, don't care.
Her eyes chuckled
and gaily the bunting danced.

Talacre Beach

Beneath the dunes we lie,
late sun bright in our closed eyes,
breeze whispering through marram grass,
sea holly, wild pansies,
tide murmuring beyond the lighthouse,
a single bird singing aloft,
a skylark surely.

A shadow falls
and we open our eyes to find
a Rhodesian Ridgeback standing over us
curiously. A moment later
he's off up the beach
after his master
without so much as a yelp.

Opening my eyes again I'm puzzled
by the bubbles,
a billion at least,
pale cloud beyond. Microscopic
bubbles, like snowflakes falling.
I see them clearly,
follow them easily,
though she cannot see them at all.

Footprints in the sand:
paw prints, claw prints,
booted feet and naked.
A long bare foot with toes both ends.
No trick of the light this time,
nor my dodgy eyesight,
but real as the Ridgeback.

She sees it too
as we walk the beach
together in joy.

Contrasts

Poet Alone

A loner –
porcelain eyes, as if on wires,
guide his floating face
above the concourse
as he hacks his way
obsessively
through the jungles of his mind,
his talent his machete.

Soon –
a clearing opens before him
and there is the crowd.
But what will they care
for his poem?

AUTHOR'S NOTE: This one stems from 40-odd years ago,
when I began writing seriously on a small mechanical
typewriter. I knew no one in the literary world back then, and
had no knowledge of the small press magazines that might have
taken my work. I submitted to the top magazines with the
inevitable result – rejection after rejection.

Sputnik

A crescent,
scabrous breasts of wanton concrete.

Political posters flap,
the tattered garments of a ravaged whore.

Dark shades,
bomber-jackets,
caps back-to-front:

"Sputnik you want? Sputnik you want?"

Banknotes crackle and packets are passed,
orange-rimmed packets of dreams.

Blades in back pockets.

Do they ever raise their gaze
above this flabby grey torso
to follow an airliner
in and out of clouds
and over the hills beyond?

Doubt it.

AUTHOR'S NOTE: "Sputnik" was a type of hashish peddled in the UK in the 1980s, when this poem was set.

City Siren

A city full of leaves,
A city full of snow.
A poet who looks like a gangster,
A gangster who looks like a poet.
The wail of a siren.
Flashing lights.
New life,
New death.

Royal Flush

High flier,
at wits' end before weekend,
savagely blasphemous on the sly.

Friday evening,
blackthorn replacing briefcase,
the slack river slackens his mind.

Foliage breaking,
the late sun stabs his eye,
a bursting shell on the Somme.

More shells,
through brain-haze wailing,
a cape of carnage poppy-field trailing.

L'Estaminet,
bitter coffee, poker, smoky stove,
he spreads a royal flush and wins.

Reverie dashed,
he wanders amongst the big watery blooms
of his cottage garden.

Indoors again,
brandy, Rachmaninov,
a fragrant wood coils at his chisel's tip.

Patiently, beneath the stair,
within buckled briefcase lair,
awaits the temptress Fortune.

Bandage

Two sad women waiting,
bloke with iPad fiddling.
Wintry sunshine through a skylight,
landscape on the wall.

My turn at last.
A tweedy, jovial doctor:
he examines it,
squashes it,
tells me not to mess with it,
just wait for it to go.

And now it has:
my blister has burst,
messily,
and a bulbous bandage
encases my right index finger,
a barrage balloon,
a blue whale,
a flock of starlings
under the moon,
one hundred thousand strong.

I cannot bend my finger,
can hardly hold my pen,
yet write this poem I will.
Bet on it, Doc:
for those brave glossy starlings,
I will.

Cat Minding

Two cats jittery indoors:
Ray sprays in a corner,
Tess drags her fur in fear.
They miss their mum.

Snores beneath loggia outside,
happy dreams of blossoming love.
Ants swarm over a fallen book
and up a hairy leg.

Tanka

Divine radiance
the warrior-poet cocooned,
wise blue eyes aflame...

Hearts and swallows gravel-drawn
his bodhrán becomes a heartbeat.

Bipolar

A pair of hot air balloons drift slowly up the river valley. What was it about her that made him smile like that? The church bell falls silent and now the doves take up their cooing again. Lambs butt heads and tug their mums; another hour and they'll be clustered in the hollows. She'd told him he had the most wonderful smile, a prelude to tapping him for a donation, he'd thought.

It wasn't that she was especially attractive or anything. She was just another collection box rattler accosting pedestrians on the High Street. Except that she wasn't actually carrying a collection box. "If I take money, I'll be arrested," she said, her confidential tone belied by a certain impishness.

The first balloon climbs on a tongue of flame, the second now following, the roar of their burners little marring the evening calm at this range. Her hi-vis tabard bore the name of a cancer charity he hadn't heard of before. Was she after a pledge or something? She wasn't even carrying leaflets. "I'm bipolar," she said.

She told him how the charity had supported her uncle in his last months; they'd been truly marvellous. He told her about his work with the homeless. It was mid-day, sunny, the High Street bustling with shoppers and workers out for lunch. He'd helped battered wives. She'd been a battered wife herself, in and out of refuges. He was retired now. She thanked him for everything he'd done for women like her. "Such a lovely smile," she sang. "Such a lovely town." And like a gambolling lamb, skipped into the crowd.

The hot air balloons reflect the last rays of the sun as they drift away upriver. She was from the city so it's unlikely he'll see her again. But remember her he will, her teasing, pleading eyes and comical way. He'll check out the website later and maybe pop a tenner on, maybe a ton.

Haiku

flood-water moon
rockets greet the New Year
old friendship revived

~~

guitars in harmony,
tapping boots not,
her voice they follow through stars

Young Ones

Granny Red

Another one sails up in a skirl of buggy wheels. "Hiya, hiya," to the mums. "Hiya," to Tom.

Big soft Tom is popular with the mums, unlike the grizzled geezer with a bald crown. He'd chance a greeting himself – course he would – if only they'd meet his eye. It makes him feel an oddity... no, invisible.

Perched on the weathervane, a rook calls over the schoolyard, its raucous cry tripping into something nearly speech, something nearly the jabber of the clustered mums.

As the bell rings for home time (or park time, as it is for most of the kids), he becomes aware of a woman at his side. She's about his own age, pretty in her day, now blond-on-grey, a granny in a red coat. Her smile is timorous, his grin almost foolish. Their granddaughters are best friends. And here they come now with their bags and lunchboxes, his little goblin and her little princess, all in a rush to be scooped up and twirled around.

Week after week, at the village park, Goblin and Princess scream delightedly as he propels them into orbit in the basket-swing. He has a bad back, so it's a relief when they join their mates racing this way and that, like starlings. It's now that Geezer and Granny Red enjoy a good chat.

Back in the sixties they danced in the same clubs, maybe even danced together, who knows? They share a passion for local history and a passion for books. And when the winter comes, bringing snow, bringing fieldfares into gardens, they discover a common interest in birds. Often they have a laugh – oh yes, they have their private jokes!

The seasons have changed and changed again since their last time together. Princess is at a new school now; Goblin has other good friends. Occasionally he'll glimpse red and spin…his almost foolish grin dying slowly. A rook calls over the park as shadows gather and one by one the mums depart in a skirl of buggy wheels. "Seeya, seeya… Seeya later, Tom."

Geezer and Goblin will stop until dusk. They're having the time of their lives.

Pollyanna-Dubček

She wears red tights, red shoes, and kicks in glee as he trundles her up the track. The pain in his back is fierce as he stoops over the buggy.

The bald man calls her Dumpling. She calls him Manma. "Pollyanna-Dubček" is a Manma/Dumpling thing.

Down the valley, early lambs sniff each ewe for a particular scent. Dumpling loves their spindly legs, their ears pink in the sun.

Pollyanna-Dubček, Pollyanna-Dubček...

***

Gulls peck over the furrows and she screws her face up in disgust. Moist black furrows, slimy furrows, half-worms wriggling – "Yuck!" says Dumpling.

Manma laughs, coughs, gasps for breath and stretches to ease his back.

Molehills at the village park – "Yuck!"

A big blue dummy in the mouth of Blond George – "Yuck!"

Pollyanna-Dubček, Pollyanna-Dubček...

***

Bald Manma grits his teeth against the pain as he pushes her on the swing...*ninety-eight-argh, ninety-nine-argh, One Hundred!*

From in front, crouching – *argh-one, argh-two, argh-three...*

Dumpling giggles, rosy-cheeked, and kicks in glee. Her red shoes thump his chest. It's all in the fun of the game.

With every push, the dry hinges squeal their familiar message:

Pollyanna-Dubček, Pollyanna-Dubček, Pollyanna...

***

Next, the basket-ride, her favourite. Dumpling is tired now, by the third revolution snoozing gently. Her tussled hair and red shoes are just visible over the green rope rim.

Manma plonks himself on a bench to wait. The sweetness of spring soothes his lungs, the sun smooths his knotted spine.

Distantly the swing squeals again, Blond George pushed by his mum. No more a message for them here than in the squabble of treetop crows. This is a Manma/Dumpling thing.

Pollyanna-Dubček, Pollyanna-Dubček, Pollyanna...

The Pole

I could do it,
I could walk along the pole,
the old telegraph pole
that lay on the ground.

Arms wide for balance,
one foot gingerly placed
in front of the other,
grandchildren following,
giggling,
I could walk along the pole,
the old telegraph pole on the ground.

Half-covered in moss
and fallen leaf,
the pole is rotten now,
yet still I glimpse
their nimble spirits
briefly.

Aguila Gigante
(a story for older children)

Joaquin was a skinny boy with a Big Dream. He lived in a faraway, Spanish-speaking country many years ago. He was an only child, twelve last birthday, and lived with Mamá in a tumbledown adobe house on the edge of the desert. They were very poor.

Joaquin didn't mind going hungry but minded very much that Mamá went hungry too. He didn't mind the pantiles leaking over his bed during the Monsoon but minded very much that Mamá got soaked as well. Mamá should be wearing filmy chiffon with a folding fan in one hand to cool her cheeks.

Papá was a brave and handsome man with a droopy moustache who'd died in the Revolution. So it was up to Joaquin now to take care of Mamá. He was learning the craft of carpentry, like Papá before him. But he had a Big Dream too, the same Big Dream that Papá once had. Joaquin dreamt of making his name as a photographer and earning lots of money, so he could give Mamá a better life in the city.

Papá had scrimped and saved to buy an expensive German camera because only good pictures would do. With its steel frame and leather bellows, you'd think it a comical camera these days, but Joaquin felt like a proper photographer already when he carried it into the desert on Papá's old bike. Someday soon he'd take a picture so amazing he'd be famous.

Of course, you could wander the desert your whole life through and never find such a shot. But Joaquin knew exactly what he was looking for, and where in the desert he might find it…

It was a dangerous mission for sure. But Joaquin had inherited more from Papá than his camera, his bicycle and his Big Dream; he'd inherited Papá's brave spirit too. Joaquin was determined to take the first ever photograph of **Aguila Gigante** – the legendary Giant Eagle.

***

In the northern part of the desert, rising high, was a red rock butte called Pancho's Hat. This was where the skinny boy in a sombrero was heading on an old sit-up-and-beg bicycle with clanking chain. A camera case was slung across his back.

Pedalling steadily in second gear, Joaquin was careful to avoid the prickly pear cacti.

He had a puncture repair kit in his saddlebag along with tools, a wrapped chicken leg with peppers, a powerful catapult and a glass jar with perforated lid for collecting small reptiles. But this would be a bad place to have his tyres popped by the prickly pear; the very worst place to stop and carry out repairs. This was **la Zona de la Muerte** – the Death Zone.

Hidden in every crevice were venomous scorpions and snakes and tarantulas. Larger predators prowled the underbrush. And a bird as black as pitch, a bird of vast wingspan with the most terrible talons and hooked bill, hunted from the sky above – *Aguila Gigante*.

Only last month an elderly traveller had been plucked from his mule's back and carried off by a Giant Eagle; carried off to its eyrie high on Pancho's Hat and fed to its monstrous chicks. So claimed the nomads of the desert anyway.

The heat was ferocious and the desert shimmered before Joaquin's sweat-stung eyes. His brain boiled beneath his sombrero. Yet still he kept going, forcing the pedals round, chain clanking. He feared the clutch of giant talons on his bony shoulders.

***

At midday the sky turned purple and a rumble of thunder sounded from somewhere beyond the mountains. Joaquin took a swig from his water bottle and wobbled to a halt, curiosity overcoming fear. There was something lodged between the twin-trunks of an ancient juniper tree. What could it be?

Gingerly he parted the tangle of foliage and berries. It was a book! An old calf-bound volume with gilt lettering on the spine. He let out a whoop of glee for it was that classic of Spanish literature *Don Quixote* by Cervantes. Maybe it had lain there abandoned for a century or more?

Too late it occurred to Joaquin that his whoop had been virtually a "come-and-get-me" cry to all the savage beasts of *la Zona de la Muerte*. He had to get away…

He grabbed the book from between the twin-trunks and recoiled with a shriek as a dozen bug-eyed lizards swarmed up his arm.

They were only tiny creatures, though – banded geckos. And with a swipe of his sombrero, Joaquin scooped one for the jar, to keep as a pet.

Something howled in the underbrush. Then came another flash of lightning, another clap of thunder: the storm was coming his way.

Prisa, prisa, thought Joaquin – hurry, hurry…

And he would have jumped back on Papá's bike had it not been for the rattle...

A scaly serpent was coiling sinuously between the spoked wheels with a chicken leg in its mouth. It was a rattlesnake, a large diamondback rattler, and it had dragged Joaquin's lunch from the saddlebag.

But now, dropping the chicken leg, the snake reared up in a tight twist, the rattle at the end of its tail vibrating madly. The small eyes in its small head were fixed on Joaquin, its forked tongue flicking in and out of its mouth, between deadly fangs. The boy was paralysed with terror as the rattler made ready to strike.

Poor Mamá, how would she cope without him?

That was the moment when, with *yips* and *yaps*, the coyotes had attacked, two of them, like small yellowish wolves.

They took the rattler from behind in a frenzy of snapping jaws. And then they were gone! They'd turned tail, whimpering, and bolted back into the wilderness, one with the thrashing snake still between its teeth, the other carrying the chicken leg.

Joaquin was stunned. He'd been sure that after finishing off the rattler, the coyotes would turn on him. Something had spooked them, obviously. Something had spooked them badly...

***

Mulberry clouds were thickening around the top of Pancho's Hat and there was a stuffy, electric feel to the air. Heart thumping, Joaquin surveyed the darkening desert...nothing.

Nothing he could see anyway...

But Joaquin was alert in every fibre, his life depending on it. And yes, surely there was the sound of stealthy movement? And a sharpening of the odour of the creosote bushes? Something was creeping through the creosote towards him, something big and powerful and hungry...

Slowly, very slowly, Joaquin reached for the catapult in his saddlebag. He slotted a stone into the pouch and drew it back as far as the elastic would stretch. *Vamos, vamos,* he thought, *Come on, come on,* willing the beast to break cover.

But he was wrong. The growl came from fifty paces to his right, not from the creosote thicket.

Joaquin swung the catapult round as the mountain lion began to sprint. He steadied his aim, fired, and missed.

A thunderclap stopped the lion in its tracks just long enough for Joaquin to reload the catapult and fire again...

Another miss, almost. The stone clipped the big cat's ear, and with a roar of injured pride it veered away towards the red rock butte.

***

He was alive anyway and thanked the Lord for that. After the rattler, the coyotes and the mountain lion, it was a miracle.

As for his Big Dream...maybe that was all it was: a dream. As for Giant Eagles...maybe it was all made up, a tale of the desert nomads, local folklore, nothing more. Oh well, he had that wonderful book, *Don Quixote*. And the bug-eyed gecko, of course. He'd call his gecko Cervantes after the great author. He'd become a carpenter of skill like Papá. He'd never be rich but the pesos he earned would suffice. He'd do his best for Mamá.

A drop of rain wet his cheek. The noontime desert was dark and stale beneath the press of clouds. Thunder rumbled.

More drops: they were plopping down on his sombrero and smacking the fat spiny pads of the prickly pear. Time to go.

Joaquin mounted Papá's old bike. The chain clanked reassuringly.

Then he found himself scrabbling in the sand, witless with fear. He'd fallen off.

Joaquin had fallen off the bike because of a call from aloft, the like of which he'd never heard before in his life: a low, soft, crooning call of terrible quivering power – a call he recognised instinctively...

And there it was, hovering in the overcast on wings of vast span, the man-eating eagle of legend, the cruellest bird in the world, black as pitch – *Aguila Gigante*.

He snatched the camera from its case but had no time to take proper aim before the Giant Eagle swooped. The down-rush of air knocked him sideways as the shutter-release clicked under his thumb. Then *C-R-A-C-K*, the world vanished in a flash of searing blue light.

Joaquin came to groggily as the juniper tree blazed in the rain. Of *Aguila Gigante*, there was no sign, save for three black tail feathers in the prickly pear, each as long as the boy was tall.

***

Years ago, before the Revolution, Papá had built a lean-to on the side of the old adobe house. He'd equipped it as a darkroom. And here it was, that evening, that Joaquin developed his photograph.

Rain drummed on the tin roof and dripped down his neck. He had only a dim red lamp for illumination in the cobwebby darkness. Yet surely *he* was glowing too, glowing with the blood-rush of his thudding heart as the black-and-white image emerged in the developing tray.

Dios Mío! He thought: Oh my God!

Joaquin felt dizzy. It was truly a shot in a million. A shot exceeding the wildest hopes of his Big Dream. For there was *Aguila Gigante*, caught in mid-swoop, steely talons outstretched and eyes ablaze with the certainty of a kill. And there, lancing through the tail of the Giant Eagle to strike the juniper below, was a blinding, zigzagging thunderbolt.

"Mamá, ay Mamá," he called hoarsely, tripping over the step, *"deberán llevar gasa!"*

"Mamá, oh Mamá, you shall wear chiffon!"